T. REX

LEIGH ROCKWOOD

PowerKiDS press

New York

Published in 2012 by The Rosen Publishing Group, Inc.
29 East 21st Street, New York, NY 10010

First Edition

Editor: Joanne Randolph
Book Design: Kate Laczynski

Photo Credits: Cover, title page by Brian Garvey; cover background (palm tree leaves) © www.iStockphoto.com/dra_schwartz; cover background (palm tree trunk) iStockphoto/Thinkstock; cover background (ginkgo leaves) Hemera/Thinkstock; cover background (fern leaves) Brand X Pictures/Thinkstock; cover background (moss texture) © www.iStockphoto.com/Robert Linton; pp. 4–5, 6, 8, 10, 11 (top, bottom), 12, 13 (top), 14–15, 16, 17, 18, 19 © 2011 Orpheus Books Ltd.; p. 7 (left) © www.iStockphoto.com/Ioan Sebastian Nicolae; p. 7 (right) © www.iStockphoto.com/Linda Steward; p. 9 © www.iStockphoto.com/Roman Ponomarets; p. 13 (bottom) © www.iStockphoto.com/Wesley Pohl; p. 20 © www.iStockphoto.com/Jello5700; p. 21 Oil Scarff/Getty Images; p. 22 Gabriel Bouys/AFP/Getty Images.

Library of Congress Cataloging-in-Publication Data

Rockwood, Leigh.
  T. Rex / by Leigh Rockwood. — 1st ed.
      p. cm. — (Dinosaurs ruled!)
  Includes index.
  ISBN 978-1-4488-4964-2 (library binding) — ISBN 978-1-4488-5078-5 (pbk.) —
  ISBN 978-1-4488-5079-2 (6-pack)
  1. Tyrannosaurus rex—Juvenile literature. I. Title. II. Series.
  QE862.S3R5555 2012
  567.912'9—dc22

                                                    2010048081

Manufactured in the United States of America

CPSIA Compliance Information: Batch #WS11PK: For Further Information contact Rosen Publishing, New York, New York at 1-800-237-9932

CONTENTS

MEET THE T. REX

The *Tyrannosaurus rex* was a large, powerful dinosaur. This hunter had a 4-foot- (1 m) long **jaw** that it used to bite into its **prey**. Its jaw was powerful enough to crush any bones that got in the way. The name *Tyrannosaurus rex* means "tyrant lizard king." A tyrant is someone who rules by force. The *Tyrannosaurus rex* is often called T. rex as a nickname.

Fossils of T. rex skeletons have given **paleontologists** clues about how the dinosaur lived, what it ate, and how it died. These clues help scientists come up with theories, or ideas, about this animal that has been **extinct** for millions of years.

Tyrannosaurus rex was one of the top predators in its prehistoric home. This dinosaur had sharp teeth and powerful jaws.

THE LATE CRETACEOUS PERIOD

Geologic time is a system that paleontologists use to make a timeline of Earth's history. It is made up of many different periods. The T. rex lived in the Late Cretaceous period. This period lasted from about 89 to 65 million years ago.

The **climate** was warm and humid throughout the Cretaceous period. Flowering plants became a big part

DINO BITE

At the beginning of the Cretaceous period, the continents were just two landmasses. When the Cretaceous period ende? most of the continents had separated.

During the Late Cretaceous period, there were many kinds of dinosaurs. Some ate meat and some ate plants.

"Cretaceous" comes from creta, which is Latin for "chalk." Chalk is a type of limestone rock that formed during this time.

of the already plentiful plant life. There were more dinosaurs during the Late Cretaceous period than there were at any other time in Earth's history.

The Late Cretaceous period ended with the mass extinction of dinosaurs. Paleontologists are not sure why this extinction happened. Their ideas about the cause include **asteroids** hitting Earth, **volcanic eruptions**, and climate change.

WHERE DID THE T. REX LIVE?

The T. rex lived mostly in what is now the western United States and southwestern Canada. Fossils of the T. rex and other Late Cretaceous plants and animals have been found in **sedimentary rocks** in these places. In the Late Cretaceous period, these lands were warm, humid, and thickly forested. Paleontologists have found fossils that show that these

Here you can see the kind of habitat in which the T. rex and other dinosaurs and reptiles from the time may have lived.

forests were filled with **conifers**, ferns, palms, and flowering plants.

The T. rex lived in this habitat with many other animals, such as the plant-eating parasaurolophus.

The habitat was a good place for plant eaters to find food. This made it a good place for the T. rex to find plant-eating prey to eat!

Some of the flowering plants that first appeared during the Late Cretaceous period were magnolias, laurels, barberries, some early sycamores, and palm trees.

T. REX BODY

An adult T. rex was about 15 to 20 feet (5–6 m) tall and about 40 feet (12 m) long from head to tail. Its strong tail helped the T. rex keep its balance while chasing its prey. The T. rex had two arms that would have been too short for it to grab prey with them. They were too short even for a T. rex to catch itself with them if it fell over.

DINO BITE

Did you know that the are fossils not only o dinosaur bones, but also of their eggs an even their poop? A pi of fossilized dinosau waste is more proper known as a coprolite

The T. rex had powerful legs and tiny arms with two fingers. Some scientists think it used its small arms to hold prey that was trying to get away.

The T. rex had four toes on its legs. Each toe had a sharp claw, as you can see here.

Paleontologists have guessed that the T. rex could run up to 15 miles per hour (24 km/h). The T. rex was covered in tough, scaly skin that looked a bit like an alligator's. Scientists know this because they have found fossilized bits of T. rex skin!

The hard parts of dinosaurs are the most likely to be fossilized. However, scientists have been lucky to find fossilized skin from a T. rex, so they have more information about how it looked.

BIG TEETH

The T. rex's teeth were huge and sharp. Its powerful jaw let this dinosaur eat both the meat and bones of its prey.

The T. rex's 4-foot- (1 m) long jaw held around 60 cone-shaped teeth. These teeth had sawlike edges. Its teeth could be more than 6 inches (15 cm) long! The T. rex shed the crowns of its teeth and grew them back about once a year. This likely helped make sure the T. rex's teeth were sharp enough to bite into prey.

The T. rex's big, sharp teeth could easily bite into prey and rip its flesh. In fact, the T. rex's jaws were so strong the dinosaur could crush its prey's bones!

These are fossilized teeth from a smaller relative of the tyrannosaurus, the Albertosaurus. Can you see the cone shape and the small curve, or bend, in the teeth?

T. REX SENSES

Paleontologists believe that all of the T. rex's senses were sharp. The dinosaur had a good sense of smell, good hearing, and good eyesight. All of these things would have been important for a **predator** like the T. rex. The dinosaur needed all the information it could get to hunt and catch its next meal.

Imagine these eyes looking at you as you were eating your lunch. The T. rex is thought to have had great eyesight, which helped it hunt well.

The T. rex likely hunted mainly using its eyes. Like most meat-eating dinosaurs, the T. rex's eyes were in the front of its head, not on the sides. With both eyes able to focus on prey, the T. rex could tell how far away that prey was. This is called **depth perception**. Dinosaurs that had eyes on the sides of their heads had poor depth perception.

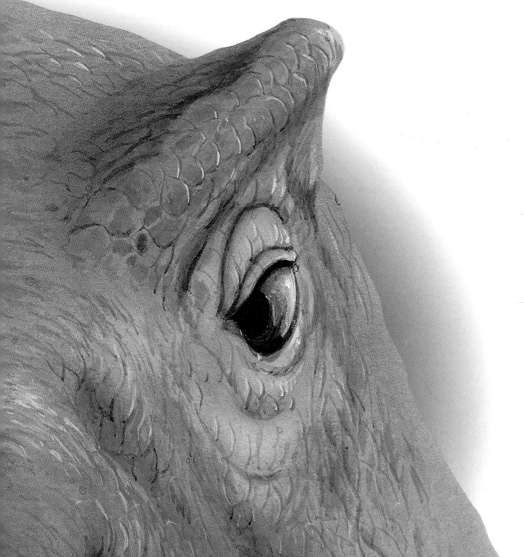

DINO BITE

Most plant-eating dinosaurs had eyes on the sides of their heads. This helped them see predators moving toward them from both sides.

A MEAT-EATING DINOSAUR

The T. rex was a **carnivore**. This means that it was a meat eater. The T. rex ate mostly plant-eating dinosaurs. Paleontologists theorize that the T. rex was likely a hunter as well as a **scavenger**. A scavenger is an animal that eats animals that are already dead when it finds them.

The T. rex likely hunted and killed other dinosaurs, such as the triceratops. Scientists think the triceratops may have tried to fight off the T. rex. It did not always succeed, though.

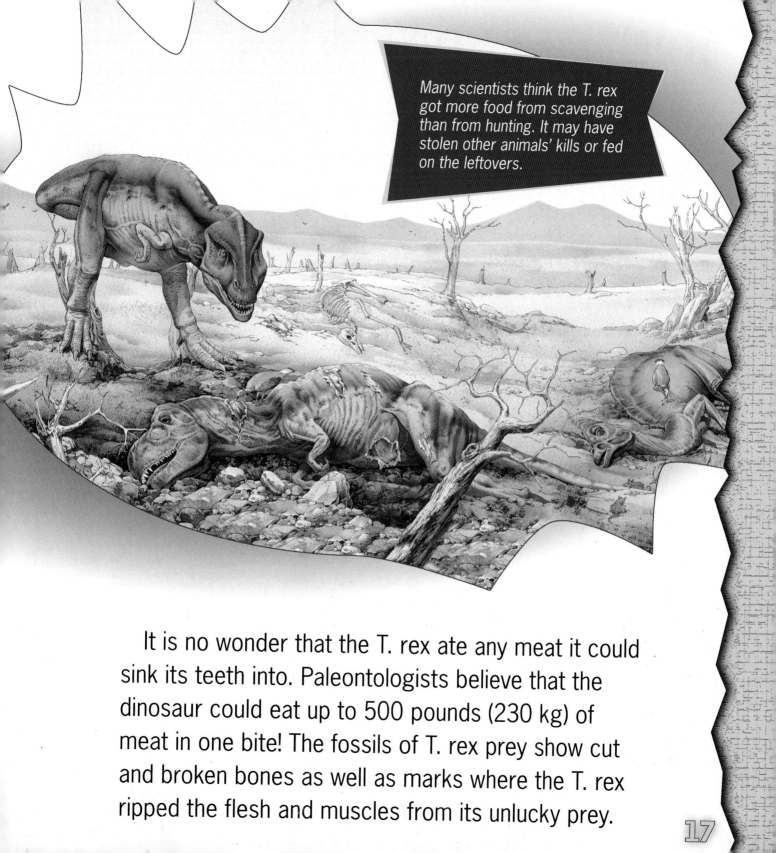

Many scientists think the T. rex got more food from scavenging than from hunting. It may have stolen other animals' kills or fed on the leftovers.

It is no wonder that the T. rex ate any meat it could sink its teeth into. Paleontologists believe that the dinosaur could eat up to 500 pounds (230 kg) of meat in one bite! The fossils of T. rex prey show cut and broken bones as well as marks where the T. rex ripped the flesh and muscles from its unlucky prey.

HUNTER AND FIGHTER

Paleontologists theorize that each T. rex hunted alone. They think this because so far there have been no fossil clues to suggest the dinosaur hunted in packs. There are clues that show that T. rexes fought each other, though. Scientists have uncovered T. rex skull fossils that look as though they have bite marks that came from another T. rex.

The T. rex was a fierce dinosaur. Can you imagine a fight between two of these huge reptiles?

Most dinosaurs would likely have tried to run or hide if they heard or saw a T. rex coming. Those unlucky enough to still be around might end up as lunch.

The reasons for these bite marks give paleontologists another mystery to solve. T. rexes could have fought each other for many reasons. The dinosaurs might have fought over **territory**, over **mates**, or over food. The T. rex could even have hunted and ate its own kind.

GROWTH AND LIFE SPAN

The rings on a tree stump show that tree's rate of growth and its age. Scientists have looked at T. rex bones under a microscope and have found rings that tell about the dinosaur's life, much as tree rings do!

They found that a T. rex was only about 10 pounds (4.5 kg) when it hatched from its egg. A T. rex grew

Scientists try to put dinosaur skeleton fossils, such as this one of a T. rex, together in a way that makes sense. The bones tell them how big the dinosaur might have been, how it might have walked, and more.

These T. rex models were made based on the latest scientific data about the T. rex. Here they show an adult T. rex and a young one side by side.

the most during its teen years. It grew about 4.5 pounds (2 kg) each day during those years! A T. rex reached its full 6-ton (5 t) size around age 18. The longest-lived T. rex that has been found was 28 years old when it died. Paleontologists think this dinosaur was near the upper limit of the T. rex's life span.

NO BONES ABOUT IT

How do scientists get T. rex fossils ready to show at a museum? When paleontologists find fossilized bones, they first carefully cut away extra rock. Then they record which bones they have found and in what position they had been lying. Then they pack up the fossils and send them to their lab to study. They then make casts, or copies, of the bones.

These paleontologists from the Natural History Museum of Los Angeles County are working on a fossil from a T. rex called Thomas.

Scientists then put together the T. rex's skeleton. They use the bones they found. They also use casts of bones from other T. rexes to take the place of missing bones. Only about 30 T. rex skeletons have ever been found. None of them are full skeletons. Each new T. rex skeleton found gives paleontologists more information about these long extinct dinosaurs.

GLOSSARY

asteroids (AS-teh-roydz) Small bodies made of rock and iron that travel around the Sun.

carnivore (KAHR-neh-vor) An animal that eats other animals.

climate (KLY-mit) The kind of weather a certain place has.

conifers (KAH-nih-furz) Kinds of trees that have needlelike leaves and grow cones.

depth perception (DEPTH per-SEP-shun) The ability to see how near or far away objects are.

extinct (ek-STINGKT) No longer existing.

fossils (FO-sulz) The hardened remains of dead animals or plants.

jaw (JAH) The bones in the top and bottom of the mouth.

mates (MAYTS) Male and female animals that come together to make babies.

paleontologists (pay-lee-on-TAH-luh-jists) People who study things that lived in the past.

predator (PREH-duh-ter) An animal that kills other animals for food.

prey (PRAY) An animal that is hunted by another animal for food.

scavenger (SKA-ven-jur) An animal that eats dead things.

sedimentary rocks (seh-deh-MEN-teh-ree ROKS) Stones, sand, or mud that has been pressed together to form rock.

territory (TER-uh-tor-ee) Land or space that animals guard for their use.

volcanic eruptions (vol-KA-nik ih-RUP-shunz) When magma comes through cracks in Earth's crust.

INDEX

WEB SITES

Due to the changing nature of Internet links, PowerKids Press has developed an online list of Web sites related to the subject of this book. This site is updated regularly. Please use this link to access the list:
www.powerkidslinks.com/dinr/trex/